Gifted-and-Talen...

'The Big Picture'

Teachers' & Parents' Guide

| Discover | Ability for Achievement
Talent for Targets
Potential for Performance |

The idea of Gifted-and-Talented students has recently been widened. 'Gifted-and-talented' is no longer simply a recognition of excellence—although this is still an important factor. Gifted-and-Talented provision now considers potential as well as performance.

'Gifted-and-Talented' provision, therefore, includes any student who has ability—particularly those students who have ability but often don't realise/apply it. New Gifted-and-Talented provision encourages schools to have a more considered attitude to 'talent', and include those students who have ability which has not been recognised in the traditional classroom setting.

What can I do as a teacher/parent....?

As a teacher/parent, you can:

1. use 'The 6 Types of Learner' to help you recognise your students' type(s)

2. read the pages on 'How to recognise the 6 types in lessons' to help you students in lessons/at home with potential gifts and talents

3. read the pages on 'How to help the 6 types'. These pages give simple strategies to support students in lessons and at home

© Kija Ltd 2008

Simple Classroom Strategies to to help Gifted-and-Talented Students

The Natural
Gift: intuition
Let them start when they're ready
Why…? Because 'naturals' just 'get it' and learn in 'space'

The 'How…?' personality
Talent: problem-solving
Give them 'steps' to follow (e.g. 1, 2, 3, etc.)
Why…? Because 'How…?' personalities need a system

The Dreamer
Talent: creative thinking
Allow them to scribble/doodle if needed
Why…? Because this is the way they learn—*internally*

The Silent Worker
Gift: internal motivation
Have 'silent-working time' in each lesson
Why…? Because silent workers need silence to think

The Talker
Talent: verbal communication
Give specific 'talk' time
Why…? Because extended silence makes talkers uneasy

The 'Why…?' personality
Gift: maturity
Give a reason (not "Because I said so.")
Why…? Because 'Why?' personalities are mature and question

Contents Page

Page 3.   The 6 Types of Gifted-and-Talented Student

Page 4.   How to recognise 'The Natural' in lessons

Page 5.   How to help 'The Natural' in lessons

Page 6.   How to recognise The 'How....?' personality in lessons

Page 7.   How to help The 'How....?' personality in lessons

Page 8.   How to recognise 'The Dreamer' in lessons

Page 9.   How to help 'The Dreamer' in lessons

Page 10.   How to recognise 'The Silent Worker' in lessons

Page 11.   How to help 'The Silent Worker' in lessons

Page 12.   How to recognise 'The Talker' in lessons

Page 13.   How to help 'The Talker' in lessons

Page 14.   How to recognise The 'Why....?' personality in lessons

Page 15   How to help 'The 'Why....?' personality in lessons

Gifted & Talented Pupils.
The 6 Types.

'The 'natural'	Gift: <u>Intuition</u> This type of student just 'gets it'.
The Student that asks "How"?	Talent: <u>problem-solving</u> This type of student likes 'steps' to follow.
'The Dreamer'	Talent: <u>creative thinking</u> This type of student needs 'space' to think.
The Silent Worker	Gift: <u>internal motivation</u> This type of student has natural desire.
The Talker	Talent: <u>verbal communication</u> This type of students needs conversation.
The Students who asks 'Why?"	Gift: <u>maturity</u> This type of students needs to know "why?".

How to recognise 'The Natural'

Gift: intuition

1. <u>The Natural</u> often sits in the centre of the classroom. <u>Why...?</u> It puts them 'in line' with the teacher and 'out-of-line' of talkers who distract them

2. <u>The Natural</u> is often quiet in lessons and doesn't offer to answer questions. <u>Why...?</u> They can be naturally shy and quietly confident and don't rely on teacher-approval because they 'get it'. <u>So...?</u> So don't insist that they 'get more involved in lessons'. This will only frustrate them.

3. <u>The Natural</u> will write/say/think things that you haven't thought of. <u>Why...?</u> Unlike the majority of students, they go beyond guidelines given to them. They 're-work' things because they know they learn most effectively by following their intuition. <u>So...?</u> So don't insist they do it 'your way'. This will only de-motivate them.

===

Possible Points of Conflict with 'The Natural'

1. <u>The Natural</u> often finish tasks quickly. <u>Solution</u>: "Colour-code your work so you can see what success criteria you've included. If you've missed any, add them"

2. <u>The Natural</u> often recreates lessons/tasks to create a greater challenge. <u>Solution</u>: "Do the task *and* add your twist to it—not just your twist.

3. <u>The Natural</u> can become arrogant about others, and you. <u>Solution</u>: "You're very good at this, John but people who aren't are good at this are good at something else. Ability requires *humility* as well."

How to help 'The 'Natural' in lessons

Gift: intuition

1: allow to start when *they're* ready

<u>Why…?</u> Because this type of learner is often self-guided.

What do you say/do…?

Example:

"If you're clear about what you need to do, off you go."

"When you're clear what the success criteria is, start."

===

2: encourage them to explain *how* they've done something

<u>Why…?</u> This improves their awareness of *how* they learn.

What do you say/do…?

Example:

"Brilliant work, Scott. What skills have you used to plan…? See if you can work out two of the thinking skills you've used when I come back in five minutes. For example, you've used **association** to plan. What other skills did you use in the planning stage…?"

"Remember, Amy, if you know how you've done it, you'll know what to use if you ever get stuck. Even 'naturals' get stuck sometimes!"

How to recognize the 'How...?' personality

Talent: problem-solving

1. The 'How...?' personality often sits near the front of the class. Why...? The 'how...?' personality needs to listen to *their own 'steps'* in their head. They need quiet to do this. Sitting at the front keeps away from the noise of the talkers (sitting at the back and the side of the class). It also gives them space to think through their system because the teacher's attention will often be spent managing the 'talkers'.

2. The 'How...?' personality will rarely ask for help. Why...? The 'how...?' personality can obsess over how something 'works' and would rather struggle to work out the 'each part' because they know they're much more likely to learn and remember this way.

3. The 'How...?' personality can get frustrated with external noise because it disturbs their thought-process. Why...? Unlike 'The Dreamer', they don't get completely lost in their own internal world so are still sensitive to other forces in the classroom. So...? So 'talkers' and 'how personalities' can clash. Keeping them apart can help both types to learn more effectively.

4. The 'How...?' personality often benefits from colour-coding their work because it shows them each part of the process/stages they had to go through to 'get it'. This colour-coding technique can be really helpful for revision.

===

Possible Points of Conflict with The 'How...?' personality

1. The 'How...?' personality will often struggle to start a task if the 'steps' they need to go through aren't explained to them. Solution: If possible, write up a step-by-step guide for them to follow. This very often helps them.

How to help the 'How...?' personality in lessons

Talent: problem-solving

1: encourage to use colour to assess their work

Why...? This helps them to see the 'stages/steps' in their learning-process.

What do you say/do...?

Example:

"Brilliant. Now get some colours and colour-code each 'learning-step' you've gone through. For example, if you look here, the first thing you did was look for **repeated/similar words**. That's one 'learning-step'—color this and try and work out how many other 'steps' you've used."

"Excellent. Now create a colour-key of the success criteria. This will help to remind you of the 'ingredients' you need to use."

==

2: encourage them to use *association* in their planning

Why...? This will improve their ability to generate ideas.

What do you say/do...?

Example:

"Remember, **association** helps you to get ideas and recall 'old' knowledge. So before you say 'I can't do it', **associate** to 'drag up' what you already know and get new ideas."

How to recognise 'The Dreamer'

Talent: creative thinking

1. <u>The Dreamer</u> often sits in the centre of the classroom near the front. <u>Why?</u> External noise frustrates them and they feel *safe* near the teacher.

2. <u>The Dreamer</u> can seem 'in their own world' in lessons. They're eye aren't focused on anyone or anything in the room. Instead, they're locking in to their *internal world*. <u>How can I tell this…?</u> They're eyes will be in two positions.

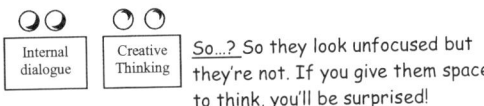

<u>So…?</u> So they look unfocused but they're not. If you give them space to think, you'll be surprised!

4. <u>The Dreamer</u> can live 'in their own world'. This need to create their own world comes from feeling like an outsider. Dreamers often have a personality trait which makes them feel different to others. Other students reinforce this. <u>So…?</u> So they 'unplug' from the world because they don't feel safe in it. Dreamers can also 'unplug' from anything which causes stress/anxiety: i.e. conflict, deadlines, sudden changes etc.

==

Possible Points of Conflict with 'The Dreamer'

1. <u>The Dreamer</u> often misses deadlines and the lies about why. <u>Solution:</u> If possible, ask them to give you the work in stages. This takes the anxiety away, probably the reason they didn't do it in the first place.

2. <u>The Dreamer</u> often works more slowly than others. <u>Solution:</u> give them 'space' to think but give also give them a *reasonable limit* you expect.

How to help 'The Dreamer' in lessons

Talent: creative thinking

<u>1:</u> get them to organize their ideas into clear 'steps'

<u>Why…?</u>   This will develop the logical side of their brains.

<u>What do you say/do…?</u>

<u>Example:</u>

T: " You've got loads of brilliant ideas, John. Which one are you going to start with?"

S: "Ummm…don't know. I never know where to start…"

T: "What if you numbered your ideas…?"

S: "Which one do I number first…?

T: "Any one you want. As long as you've got an order, you've got 'steps' to follow."

==

<u>2:</u> give them to 'space' to think.

<u>Why…?</u>   'Dreamers' often work things out *in their heads—-on their own*

<u>What do you say/do…?</u>

<u>Example:</u>

To spot a 'dreamer', look around the class for the quiet student who can be easily missed. Now, when you set a task, watch what they do. If they don't start to work straight away but seen to be 'looking off into space' silently they're probably generating ideas. Give 'space'.

How to recognise 'The Silent Worker'

Gift: internal motivation

1. <u>The Silent Worker</u> will often sit 'in opposition' to 'The Talker'. <u>Meaning…?</u> If the 'talkers' are sat at the front of the room, 'The Silent Worker' will sit at the back. If the 'talkers' are sat at the back of the room, 'The Silent Worker' will sit at the front. <u>Why…?</u> 'The Silent Worker' is affected by the slightest sound but they're also often non-confrontational because they respond to calm.

2. <u>The Silent Worker</u> often hopes for praise in lessons. <u>Why…?</u> 'The Silent Worker's' personality (quiet, polite, hard-working) means they often get 'forgotten' when a teacher is managing the 'talkers' whose need for reassurance from their friends and the teacher mean they dominate. <u>So…?</u> So 'The Silent Worker' has the same need for reassurance but it isn't made obvious because they're not talkers. <u>Meaning…?</u> They often produce more work than the other 5 types in lessons as a secret way of drawing the teacher's attention. <u>Go on…</u> Because 'The Silent Worker' always produces a lot of good work and behaves well, teachers can see this as 'what they always do'. <u>So…?</u> So 'what they always do' is outstanding but what they often don't get is the teacher saying "outstanding!".

==

Possible Points of Conflict with the Silent Worker

1. 'The Silent Worker' can become de-motivated if they're criticized for minor things. E.g. the rare times when they talk or aren't focused in lessons. <u>So, I ignore the minor off-task behaviour.</u> It helps to, because if a teacher generally doesn't comment on their regular, outstanding achievement but then jumps on the first thing they do wrong, they can think: "What's the point of trying to please them…?"

How to help 'The Silent Worker' in lessons

Gift: internal motivation

1: praise one-to-one to raise their personal profile

<u>Why...?</u> This builds self-esteem and confidence which is often low.

What do you say/do...?

Example (Science, Maths, D.T.):

" Brilliant diagrams to explain your process, Joe. Keep shining...!"

"You always give a hundred per-cent, Steph and I'm always impressed. Well done!"

"Your desire and talent doesn't go unnoticed, Tony! Keep shining.. "

===

2: use their work as an example of good practice

<u>Why...?</u> This builds their classroom-profile and, again, their confidence.

What do you say/do...?

Example (Science, Maths...):

T: "Have a look at this one by Joe. What's he done that makes his work *stand out*...?"

Class: "He's used diagrams to show his workings-out."

T: " And why does that make a difference...?"

Class: " coz it helps you to 'see' it more clearly ... "it helps you to 'get it' easier."

How to recognise 'The Talker'

Talent: verbal communication

1. The Talker often sits at the back or side of the room. Why…? They often have deep insecurities and need continual reassurance from their friends *and you*. So…? Try not to insist on long periods of silence because The Talker has a core emotional need to interact. Meaning…? Meaning The Talker's need for reassurance overrides *your* need for them to shut up!

2. The Talker finds sitting still and working quietly very difficult. They turn around and look up a lot in lessos. Why…? Sitting quietly makes The Talker feel alone and isolated. This feeling of isolation and loneliness is at the core of The Talker's insecurity. So…? So silence makes The Talker feel *vulnerable*.

3. The Talker will ask you endless questions about the lessons *and your life*. Why…? The Talker needs to form *relationships* with authority figures because often their immediate authority figures (parents/guardians) don't openly value them.

4. The Talker likes to sit within a group. Why…? This acts as their *security blanket*, making them feel *safe* and *valued*

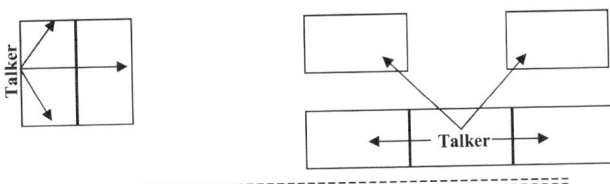

===

Possible Points of Conflict with 'The Talker'

1. Talkers often insist that they "need to talk to learn" Solution: "I know you need to talk to learn because it makes you feel secure *but* not over me and not when we're *listening as a class.*"

How to help 'The Talker' in lessons

Talent: verbal communication

1: expect conversation and humour

Why…? Talkers often need to build personal relationships.

What do they say/do…?

Example:

S: "How's it going, Sir? Have a good weekend with the family…?"

===

2: expect numerous questions (of you and others)

Why…? Talkers often use conversation to feel secure in themselves, their environment and their learning..

What do you/they say/do…?

Example (D.T.):

S: "Miss, what do I do here again,,,?"

T: "You need to check the scale of your design before you start actually making it."

S: " Okay. (20 seconds later…) John, let me have a look at yours. What's wrong with my scale…?"

S: " I dunno… maybe it's gonna be too heavy when you actually build it."

T: "Okay, Tony…? Think about the eventual *size and weight*… Off you go."

How to recognise the 'Why...?' personality

Gift: maturity

1. The 'Why...?' personality is emotionally and psychologically very mature. So...? So they don't accept authority unquestioningly. Why...? They're maturity means they see teachers (irregardless of age or position) as *people*—equals. So...? So they won't do something just because someone in authority has told them to. Why...? Fairness and mutual respect are a core part of the 'why?' personality's make-up. So...? Treat them like adults because they think and respond like one.

2. The 'Why...? personality needs to see the *personal relevance* (the 'point') of something, including lessons. Why...? Their maturity means they are able to 'project':i.e. *think beyond* school. So...? So 'why' personalities will often put lessons into a 'life' context. Meaning...? They need to see 'the point' of lessons *beyond school*.

3. The 'Why...?' personality can refuse to do something, particularly if they think they've been disrespected or ignored. Why...? Unlike other students, the 'why' personality sees school as a place full of people *not* an institution with rules that must be followed. They won't follow rules unless they personally value them. So...? So try to speak to them like adults. Try to make the 'why' personality see the 'personal value' of lessons.

==

Possible Points of Conflict with the 'Why...?' personality

1. 'Why...?' personalities often question the simplest instructions. Solution: always give them an explanation. Replying: "because I said so" won't work!

2. 'Why...?' personalities can comment on lessons inappropriately. Solution: speak to them one-to-one. "I know you don't see the point, Sarah and if you'd asked me *politely* I would have explained it. *Tone*, Sarah—*tone*."

How to help the 'Why…?' personality in lessons

Gift: maturity

1: expect to be asked "Why…?" a lot

<u>Why…?</u> "Why…?" personalities often need to see the *personal (life) relevance* of things to value them.

<u>What do you say/do…?</u>

Example (Maths):

S: "Why are we doing this…?"

T: "It's on your GCSE paper…"

S: "No. I mean *why* are we doing it…? When am I gonna use Algebra…?"

T: "Algebra's problem-solving, James and life's about solving problems. So Algebra's going to show you how *you* solve problems and how you can solve *any problem* better."

===

2: try to answer "Why…?" by giving a 'life' example

<u>Why…?</u> This is how "Why…?" personalities value things. They think *beyond* school.

<u>What do you/they say/do…?</u>

Example (Art):

T: "<u>Texture</u> is *like layering a cake*—the more layers, the sweeter the cake! Get it…?"

'Different not More' Strategies for G&T Students

Subject: Art

Choose one strategy from the examples below and add it as a PLP target

1. Use <u>complex visual</u> analysis to understand the work of others

   Example: Create a painting or sculpture using similar materials to the artist

2. Use <u>an appropriate range</u> of shading pencils

   Example: Use a HB for drawing, a 2B for mid tones and a 4B/graphite pencil for dark tones.

3. Use <u>categorisation and association</u> in analysis to gain more ideas

   Example: Study the use of rain water then use appropriate examples

   Puddles   drinking
   Mud   life

4. Use a <u>variety of mediums</u> for development in a project

   Example: Create small test pieces to show a variety of working methods.

5. Consider compositions and layouts

   Example: A portrait may be slightly off set rather than right in the middle of the paper. This will show a larger area of interest

6. Use <u>creative</u> presentation in sketchbooks and work sheets

   Example: collect appropriate papers, textures, colours etc. that can be used to creatively display (but not overcrowd) information.

'Different not More' Strategies for G&T Students

Subject: Business Studies

Choose <u>one</u> strategy from the examples below and add it as a PLP target

1. Demonstrate **knowledge and understanding** of a range of business concepts related to the unit that you are studying. **Know WHAT** you are learning. For example, use business terminology to explain concepts and scenarios. "The Boston Matrix is used by businesses to"--------

⇩

2. **Apply knowledge and understanding** to **explain** concepts and illustrate your explanation with examples from actual businesses. Know HOW businesses operate or use models to aid decisions.

For Example, "From my research this is illustrated by -----"

⇩

3. **Analyse complex business issues, problems and opportunities. Know Why BUSINESS take the action they do.**

For example: Compare similarities and differences, advantages and constraints. Use the PESTEL and SWOT models to help.

⇩

4. Evaluate and make judgements by prioritising evidence and arguments, make judgements and draw conclusions. Make recommendations and justify these. For example, "Based on my research I think the most significant issues are because ---------------"

⇩

5. Refer to the assessment criterion of <u>mark band 3</u>

<u>QWC</u> : Demonstrate quality of written communication. For example, make sure your written work uses specialist terms consistently and your response is well organised. For example, in Report format. Spelling and punctuation and grammar should be used with accuracy.

⇩

6. Link concepts and skills together, knowledge and understanding.

Increase depth and breath of understanding, increase application of knowledge and skills, increase knowledge and understanding of skills, increase synthesis and evaluation. Show independence.

'Different not More' Strategies for G&T Students

Subject: Drama

Choose <u>one</u> strategy from the examples below and add it as a PLP target

---

1

Perform a role different in <u>age</u> and <u>status</u>

Example: If you have previously played roles of a similar age to yourself, play an older character.

⬇

2

Use <u>symbols</u> in your performance work

Example: blue lighting to represent night-time; a white costume to represent the innocence of a character.

⬇

3

Take on the role of <u>director</u>

Example: Take a short section of your performance and direct it in a different style e.g. a realistic piece done in the style of Melodrama. Does this bring out ideas that can be incorporated in to your performance?

⬇

4

Lead <u>extra-curricular rehearsals</u> for the group

Set yourself and your group a target for each rehearsal.

⬇

5

Use <u>technical mediums of Drama</u> to enhance performance work

Example: Create a soundtrack for your piece including music for the beginning and end as well as incidental music and sounds.

⬇

6

Study the <u>performance of another actor</u> (either on stage or screen) and try to emulate some of their performance in your own work

Example: If performing an extract from the play 'Teechers', choose an actor from the TV programme 'Waterloo Road' who plays a similar character and study their characterisation.

'Different not More' Strategies for G&T Students

Subject: English

Choose <u>one</u> strategy from the examples below and add it as a PLP target

---

1 use <u>complex sentences</u> to improve written expression

Example: <u>**Studying the sky,**</u> the stranger continued into town

⇩

2 use <u>synonyms</u> to improve the precision of descriptions

Example: The woman **<u>sauntered</u>** past, **<u>dismissing</u>** his wave.

⇩

3 Use <u>frequent, short embedded quotations</u> in analysis

Example: Shakespeare escalates the drama in Act 3, Scene 1 with Tybalt's order to **"turn and draw"**, avenging Romeo's **"intrusion"** and acting as the catalyst for the play's tragic climax

⇩

4 Use a <u>variety of punctuation</u> for precision of expression

Example: It's funny what you remember <u>...</u> when you look back <u>–</u> look at it head-on, that is. Fear is what I remember<u>:</u> pure fear.

⇩

5 Refer to aspects of <u>form</u> for high-level analysis

Example: The opening <u>**metaphor**</u> "two tongues" establishes an immediate sense of conflict in the poem, reinforced by the <u>**extended metaphor**</u> "rot ... die ... spit it out", implying an identity crisis within the poem.

⇩

6 Use <u>segue</u> to link ends and beginnings of paragraphs

Example: The opening metaphor "two tongues" establishes an immediate sense of conflict in the poem, reinforced by the extended metaphor "rot ... die ... spit it out", implying an **<u>identity</u>** crisis within the poem.

The conflicting sense of **<u>identity</u>** is continued with the...

'Different not More' Strategies for G&T Students

Subject: FOOD

Choose <u>one</u> strategy from the examples below and add it as a PLP target

1. Make sure you have evaluated both process and outcome in practical sessions.

Example: Identify strengths weaknesses and improvements in the way you worked and what you produced. Check against assessment criteria.

2. Demonstrate that you are able to analyse, compare and evaluate information and ideas.

Example: Analyse methods of monitoring and measuring customer service, outlining the strengths and weaknesses of each.

3. Make sure you pay attention to the finish of practical work.

Example: Consider the look of the food, the garnish or decoration and the correct serving.

4. Make sure discrimination is shown throughout your work when selecting and acquiring relevant research.

Example: Before putting research into work, stop and check that its relevant and make sure it is in your own words.

5. Make sure all pieces of work are legible, easy to understand and show a good grasp of grammar, punctuation and spelling.

Example: Use a computer to producing any written work needed and get teacher to check before printing.

6. Use specialist vocabulary in written and oral work.

Example: Use the names of processes, equipment, nutrients and sensory descriptors.

'Different not More' Strategies for G&T Students

Subject: Geography

Choose <u>one</u> strategy from the examples below and add it as a PLP target

1. use <u>complex sentences</u> to improve your description skills. All good geographical answers start with a clear and accurate description. 'The environment was arid, desert stretched as far as the mountains on the horizon'.

⇩

2. use <u>explanation</u> to demonstrate your knowledge of the topic you are working on.

'The environment is arid due to the high temperature and the fact that it hasn't rained for two months'.

⇩

3. Use factual data to improve the accuracy of your statements.

'The environment is arid due to the high temperature, over 40 degrees celsius daily, and the fact that it hasn't rained for two months.'

⇩

4. Use the skill of analysis to formulate clear accurate responses to issues and dilemma's you face.

Research both sides of an argument, utilise the 5W's and How? to form the key questions in your research.

⇩

5. Refer to a variety of sources for high-level analysis

The key to successful analysis is being able to assimilate a number of different sources of information, then form an opinion. Use techniques like mind mapping and spider diagrams to gather information. They are powerful as they encourage you to classify information.

⇩

6. Have an **opinion.** Good geographers know what they think, can develop an argument and express themselves using clear accurate language.

'Different not More' Strategies for G&T Students

Subject: History.

Choose one strategy from the examples below and add it as a PLP target

1. Ensure that you have followed the command word of the question and shown the marker you have understood its demands.

Example: In comparing and contrasting sources C & D, we are able to ascertain...

⇩

2. Answer the question directly throughout the work – **you should not leave a direct response to the question until the conclusion.** You should not use the body of the answer to write down everything you've found out. Long-winded introductions that 'set the scene' should be avoided.

⇩

3. To show a higher level of understanding use your own background knowledge to contextualise and validate each point you make, in relation to the sources and the questions.

Example: When using a quotation from a source, explain its relevance to the question by referring to additional information from your own knowledge (ie. not contained in that source).

⇩

4. You should always look for the counter-argument. The examiner will try to lead you in one direction, you need to spot the missing argument and consider other directions (the counter argument).

Example: To what extent was X the main contributory factor in causing Y? Don't forget that other factors (eg. A, B or C) may also contribute or be the most significant factor.

⇩

5. You must support each judgement/point using the sources provided. Do not just take these sources as a given, using the skills of analysis and synthesis highlight issues and problems relating to the question.

⇩

6. Remember to write a strong conclusion that provides your summative judgement. Produce a **conclusion** that sums up your answer to the question. This conclusion should grow naturally from, and be consistent with, the main body of the answer. It should include some argument and support and be more than a couple of lines long.

'Different not More' Strategies for G&T Students

Subject: KS4 ICT

Choose <u>one</u> strategy from the examples below and add it as a PLP target

develop <u>detailed</u> <u>explanations</u> to <u>describe</u> the of aim of a product

Example: *All products are produced for a particular purpose. A product may have just one aim or more than one aim. When you identify the aim(s), think about whether the clip has been produced to:*

- *Provide information (e.g. product recalls by consumer agencies or manufacturer)*
- *Change behaviour (e.g. drink driving campaigns, benefit fraud, anti-smoking)*
- *Attract attention (e.g. a film sound track)*
- *Persuade the target audience to purchase a product (e.g. goods for sale)*
- *Persuade the target audience to join something (e.g. a keep fit class)*
- *Entertain (e.g. a music clip)*
- *Teach specific skills or educate (e.g. teaching foreign language skills).*

⇩

develop <u>detailed</u> <u>explanations</u> to <u>describe</u> the target audience of a product

Example: *Any type of product is created for a reason and is aimed at a specific group of people (i.e. a target audience). To be specific you need to include things like:*

- *Age group - products may be aimed at people of a certain age (e.g. teenagers)*
- *Gender – a product may be aimed at males or females.*
- *Education – a product may be aimed at people in a particular profession (e.g. medical postgraduates). A target group's level of education could influence how and what they buy.*
- *Family size – a commercial presentation for larger cars (e.g. people carriers) may be aimed at larger families.*
- *Income level – this factor is about the affordability of a product and what the product says about the wealth and income of the person (e.g. skiing holidays)*
- *Graphical location – a local newsletter is aimed at a small group of people living in a particular suburb or town.*

⇩

give a <u>thorough</u> <u>explanation</u> of the good features of a product with <u>justification</u>

Example: *The advert was very effective as it gave clear information about the dangers of smoking to one's own health as well as the harms of passive smoking. The sounds of the smoker with lung cancer struggling to breathe and the agonising crying of his young children were disturbing and thought provoking.*

⇩

'Different not More' Strategies for G&T Students

Subject: Mathematics

Choose <u>one</u> strategy from the examples below and add it as a PLP target

---

Solve problems by breaking down into smaller more manageable parts.
EXAMPLES:
(1) If 12 becomes 96, 13 becomes 117 and 15 becomes 165, what does 14 become?
(2) The sixty creepy crawlies in John's garden are made up of spiders and ants, and have a total of 406 legs? How many are spiders?

Use conventions, definitions and derived properties in geometry i.e. angles, parallel lines, triangles and polygons, all circle parts, constructions loci/shape and space.
EXAMPLE: Sketch a triangle. Draw in the bisectors of the three angles. Is it possible to draw a triangle where two of these angle bisectors are at right angles to each other? Can you prove it?
(Hint: Assume that two of the angle bisectors *do* meet at 90º. Follow through the consequences.....)

Present concise reasoned arguments/justification for answers
EXAMPLES : Is $\dfrac{7}{10}$ closer to ¾ or to ⅔?   How can you be sure?

Solve problem & represent a problem mathematically using symbols, words, diagrams and tables
EXAMPLE: Jim has three times as many comic books as Charlie. Charlie has two-thirds as many comic books as Bob. Bob has 27 comic books. How many comic books does Jim have?

Develop and use the correct vocabulary of probability -Mutually exclusivity, Independent events etc. Understand and justify - estimation from experimental compared to the theoretical.
EXAMPLE: Two eight-sided dice have sides numbered 1 through 8. Each side has the same probability of landing face up. What is the probability that the product of the two numbers on the sides that face up exceeds 36?

Plot and understand graphs of functions, including where *y* is given explicitly in terms of *x*; recognise that equations of the form $y = mx + c$ correspond to straight-line graphs. Given values for *m* and *c*, find the gradient of lines given by equations of the form $y = mx + c$.
EXAMPLEs:
(1) What happens when m gets bigger?
(2) What happens when m gets smaller?
(3) What would happen if x was negative? What would happen if x was x^2? Why?

'Different not More' Strategies for G&T Students

Subject: MFL

Choose <u>one</u> strategy from the examples below and add it as a PLP target

1. Opinions
Give your opinion whenever possible. To start with this could be a simple "I like this/ don't like this because…" As your language develops this will become more complex and could involve a justification with different tenses.

2. Synonyms
Maintain a list of synonyms which you will add to as your knowledge of vocabulary develops. Use this list to enrich your writing/ spoken language. For example instead of saying "It is important" try to use phrases like "It is essential/ vital."

3. Memory Techniques
Experiment with different memory techniques to identify the way in which you learn best. Decide how you retain information.

4. Using all your knowledge.
When writing on a specific topic try to include vocabulary and constructions from different topics. For example when writing about hobbies you could perhaps include details about what there is to do in Stouport to support these hobbies.

5. Using constructions independently.
When you are given a new construction try to change some the nouns/ verbs in there for ones of your choosing so that you are able to use this construction to say what you want to say.

'Different not More' Strategies for G&T Students

Subject: P.E.

Choose one strategy from the examples below and add it as a PLP target

1. Mark your own exam questions using mark schemes

Example: RAG the mark scheme compared to the answer that you wrote and identify ways to access additional marks.

⬇

2. For longer questions (3 Marks or more) use the PEE Method – Point, Explain, Example

Example: The Olympics in London will be a good thing for the UK as it will force the government to invest more money in building new facilities (Point). This will mean that more money will be put into sport to build training facilities and competition venues that can be used by the public once the Games have finished (Explain). This is already happening in the East End of London where new facilities such as the Olympic Stadium are being built using the money that has been provided by the government.

⬇

3. Write your own exam questions and mark scheme using the syllabus.

Example: Complete these questions yourself or swap them with a partner and test each other!

⬇

4. Test yourself on different levels of questions (e.g. 1 Mark, 3 Marks, 5 Marks)

Example: Attempt 1/2 Mark questions to check your knowledge of the content. Attempt 3/4 Mark questions to develop your ability to explain your knowledge using sporting examples. Attempt 5/6 Mark questions to develop your ability to be analytical and argue your answer from different viewpoints (e.g. positive/negative, advantages/disadvantages).

'Different not More' Strategies for G&T Students

Subject: Religious Studies.

Choose <u>one</u> strategy from the examples below and add it as a PLP target

1. Ensure you introduce the point, linking back to the question, before stating the Bible quote.

Example: Many Christians would disagree with the issue of…because in the Bible it says…

⇩

2. Use a greater number of Bible quotes to support each point of view and write a **balanced** argument in your essay answers. Try to link ideas from the different units you have studied – see the subject **holistically** rather than compartmentalised.

⇩

3. Demonstrate a greater understanding of the complications Christians face when making ethical decisions by using the same quote for both sides of the argument.

Example: Some Christians may disagree with the use of IVF because they believe their inability to conceive naturally may be 'part of God's plan, they are not meant to have children of their own'. Alternatively, other Christians believe 'God has a plan for every human life', therefore it may be part of the plan to use IVF and in order to start a family of their own.

⇩

4. Aim to explain the symbolism whenever possible, demonstrating an understanding of how Christian belief is expressed.

Example: the empty cross demonstrates a Christian belief in the resurrection of Jesus and the forgiveness of sins, allowing Christians a way back to God in heaven, saving them from the punishment of death.

⇩

5. Demonstrate an improved level of **empathy** in your writing. This will be clear to the examiner through your explanation of **why** Christians believe the things they do and how they **act** in accordance with this, written in a non - judgemental manner.

⇩

6. Remember to refer to different denominations of Christians wherever possible. We have made reference in our learning to Catholics, Church of England (Anglicans), Methodists, Baptists, Evangelical Christians, Quakers. They have different views about ethical issues for example divorce, abortion, euthanasia etc. Also in the nature of their belief e.g. their place of worship or how they worship.

'Different not More' Strategies for G&T Students

Subject: Science

Choose **one** strategy from the examples below and add it as a PLP target

1. Use scientific vocabulary and terminology to improve written answers
Example: Light refracts as it passes from one medium to another (rather than "light bends")

2. Clearly lay out all your working, including the formula or equation you are using, when performing calculations, and ensure you give units for the answer.
Example :   F = ma   Answer units = Newtons
Use formula triangles to rearrange equations for appropriate term

3. In practical work, always identify the independent and dependent variables, and whether they are continuous, discrete or categoric.

Example: Independent = Temperature (continuous)
Dependent = Rate of reaction (continuous)

4. When drawing diagrams of experimental equipment and set-ups, ensure the apparatus is complete and would work as required.
Example: Ensure boiling tube has a bung in it if a delivery tube is coming from it

5. Results tables: Always ensure independent and dependent variables in correct columns; data in numerical order; data quoted to appropriate precision; labels and units included for all variables.

Temperature (°C)	Time taken (sec)
20	
40	

6. Plotting graphs: always ensure you choose appropriate graph to display data (line or bar chart); use appropriate scales for axes; fully label axes with variable names and units; include graph title; **check plots**
Example: Height of
                Froth (mm)

                                    Mass of liver used (g)

4 give a <u>thorough</u> <u>explanation</u> of the not so good features of a product with <u>justification</u>

Example: The sound quality was very poor which meant that you as the audience has to really listen hard to the advertisement just in case you missed out on some vital piece of information. There was also an echo throughout the advert which made it difficult to hear what was being said. The clip was badly recorded and could make the listener want to change the channel.

Printed in Great Britain
by Amazon.co.uk, Ltd.,
Marston Gate.